Contents

n. track The text is recorded in full.

Before you read

1 Prediction

Put the pictures in the order that you think they will happen in Chapter One.

D

E

2 Vocabulary

Find illustrations of the following words/phrases in the pictures above.

1	a screen	4	mistletoe	7	a counter
2	green tinsel	5	a mirror	8	a road sign
3	sweating	6	a steering wheel	9	businessmen

3 Now read Chapter One and see if you put the pictures in the right order.

5

Andrea M. Hutchinson

Home for Christmas

Activities by **Laura Clyde**
Additional activities by **Robert Hill**
Illustrated by **Alessandra Scandella**

DUBL

PORT

Editors: Michela Bruzzo, Robert Hill
Design and art direction: Nadia Maestri
Computer graphics: Simona Corniola
Picture research: Laura Lagomarsino

© 2008   Black Cat

First edition : January 2008

DEALINK, DEAFLIX are trademarks licensed by
De Agostini SpA

Picture credits:
Cideb Archive; © Michael St. Maur Sheil/CORBIS: 22;
© H P Merten/Robert Harding World Imagery/CORBIS: 24;
Gary Roebuck/Alamy: 41; Shangara Sing/Alamy: 54; Janine
Wiedel Photolibrary/Alamy: 56.

We would be happy to receive your comments and
suggestions, and give you any other information
concerning our material.
info@blackcat-cideb.com
blackcat-cideb.com

CISQ CISQ CERT
TEXTBOOKS AND
TEACHING MATERIALS
The quality of the publisher's
design, production and sales processes has
been certified to the standard of
UNI EN ISO 9001

Printed in Italy by Italgrafica, Novara

CHAPTER ONE **Going Nowhere**

Harminda looked at her watch and then at the traffic outside.
The airport was 10 kilometres away and it was already 5.15 p.m.

track 02

'Isn't there a quicker way to get to the airport? My plane leaves in less than two hours,' she asked the taxi driver.

'Are you going home for Christmas?' he smiled. The taxi was full of decorations; there was green tinsel on the steering wheel and mistletoe under the mirror.

'Yes...' said Harminda. But there was no Christmas spirit in her voice.

Harminda looked out of the window, trying not to cry. She remembered the phone call from her Mum earlier that day. She missed her parents so much.

Their argument, [1] four years ago, seemed stupid now.

Thirty minutes later, they arrived at Galway airport.

1. **argument** : when people do not agree and get angry.

'How much is it?' she asked.

'Fifteen euros for you, sweetheart,' said the taxi driver with a smile.

Harminda gave him a twenty-euro note and got quickly out of the taxi.

'Don't forget your change...' shouted the taxi driver, with a five-euro note in his hand, but Harminda was already inside the airport terminal.

There were a lot of people, and Harminda pushed through the crowd to look at the screens for her flight...

'Cancelled? Stay calm and read it again, slowly. You've read it wrong, that's all,' she thought.

'Flight ZXY 247... destination, London Stansted... cancelled!'

All flights from Galway were cancelled because of bad weather.

'I'm sorry, but tomorrow's flight to London is fully booked. [1] Christmas is a busy time of year,' said the man at the ticket office when Harminda tried to find another flight.

'What about another airport? Dublin perhaps?'

'Sorry...'

'You don't understand,' said Harminda, 'I have to get to London as soon as possible. My Dad's ill.'

'I really am very sorry...' the man said sympathetically. [2] 'You could hire a car. It's a long journey, but if you need to get there quickly...'

As Harminda ran towards car hire, she saw that there were only two women waiting and she started to feel hopeful.

---

1. **fully booked :** full; there are no free places.
2. **sympathetically :** in a way that shows he knows how Harminda is feeling.

'I'm sorry, but this is the last car,' she heard the assistant say.

'But I was here first!' shouted a tall, blonde woman.

'Only because you pushed in front of me! I'm getting married in three days. I have to get to London,' shouted an Irish girl in her late twenties.

'And I've got a very important audition!' [1] said the blonde woman.

'Excuse me,' interrupted Harminda. 'Did you say that there's only one car?'

'Yes, and it's mine!' said the blonde arrogantly. [2]

'No it's not!' The argument continued.

Harminda wanted to cry. But then she had an idea.

'If you two are going to London, we can share the car! What do you think? We can share the driving and the cost.'

The two women looked at her in silence.

'They probably think I'm mad,' thought Harminda. But that didn't worry her. The only thing that worried her was getting to London to see her family.

'Well, if *you* want to get to your audition,' Harminda said to the blonde, 'and if *you* want to get married,' she said to the other woman, 'well... you've got no choice!'

Harminda was speaking angrily, and after a moment, the two women reluctantly [3] agreed.

'Mr O'Flaherty will be pleased,' thought Chrissie, the car hire assistant, as she showed the women their car.

1. **audition :** a short performance by an actor, dancer or musician to show if they are good enough for a film/show, etc.
2. **arrogantly :** in a way that shows she thinks she is more important than other people.
3. **reluctantly :** in a way that shows they don't really want to do it.

'Chrissie! Chrissie!' a man shouted, running towards them. It was very cold, but he was sweating, and his face was red and angry.

'Oh, that's my boss. Merry Christmas!' she smiled, and closed the door.

'Stop them, Chrissie!'

'What...? It's OK, Mr O'Flaherty. They've paid,' she smiled, waving at the car as it left.

'That car was reserved, you stupid girl!' he shouted.

Chrissie's face turned red. She didn't see the three businessmen as she ran into the airport, crying.

'Where is my car, Mr O'Flaherty?' asked one. His voice was calm, but his grey eyes were dangerous.

Colin O'Flaherty turned around nervously [1] to talk to the three men. And he knew that he was in trouble. Big trouble.

1. **nervously :** in a way that shows he is worried or frightened.

The text and **beyond**

KET **1** **Comprehension check**

Are these sentences 'Right' (A) or 'Wrong' (B)? If there is not enough information to answer 'Right' or 'Wrong', choose 'Doesn't say' (C). There is an example at the beginning (0).

0 Harminda has a good relationship with her parents.
  A Right   **B** Wrong   **C** Doesn't say

1 The flights to London are fully booked for the next three days.
  A Right   **B** Wrong   **C** Doesn't say

2 Harminda wants to get to London quickly to see her father.
  A Right   **B** Wrong   **C** Doesn't say

3 There are lots of cars for hire.
  A Right   **B** Wrong   **C** Doesn't say

4 The other two women agree to hire a car together.
  A Right   **B** Wrong   **C** Doesn't say

5 Mr O'Flaherty is happy that Chrissie has hired the car to the three women.
  A Right   **B** Wrong   **C** Doesn't say

6 The three businessmen are criminals.
  A Right   **B** Wrong   **C** Doesn't say

2 **Vocabulary – adverbs to show attitude**

Match the following adverbs from Chapter One to their definitions.

1 ☐ angrily   **3** ☐ nervously   **5** ☐ sympathetically
2 ☐ arrogantly   **4** ☐ reluctantly

A showing that you are doing something that you don't want to do
B showing that you are worried or frightened
C showing that you are not happy with someone/something
D showing that you understand how someone feels
E when you think that you are better or more important than other people

3 Characters

Now match an adverb from the previous task with the character who says or does something in that way. There is one extra character who you don't need to use.

A ☐☐ the tall blonde woman   **D** ☐☐ Harminda
B ☐☐ the man at the airline desk   **E** ☐☐ Chrissie
C ☐☐ the Irish girl in her late twenties   **F** ☐☐ Mr O'Flaherty

TRINITY 3

4 Speaking: the weather

The story takes place in winter, at Christmas, and snow and bad weather make travelling difficult for the three girls. Ask and answer the questions below with a partner.

- What is the weather like in winter in your country?
- Does it snow in your country? If so, do you like it when it snows?
- What's your favourite season and why?

5 London airports

Find London's five airports on the map below. Which do you think are the nearest to and the farthest from the centre of London?

1 Stansted   **2** Luton   **3** Heathrow   **4** Gatwick   **5** City

6 Listening

track 03

Listen to the information about flights and match it to the relevant passenger. There is one extra passenger. The first one has been done as an example.

A ☐ This passenger wanted to fly to Heathrow today, but can't.

B ☐ This passenger wants to change her flight from Gatwick to Heathrow.

C ☐ This passenger has got a choice of three different days of the week to fly to Luton.

D ☐ This passenger wanted to fly to London tomorrow, but can change her plans.

E ☐1 This passenger wants to go to London today. It's not important for him which airport he arrives at.

Before you read

1 Vocabulary

Match the different types of sea transport to each picture.

1 ferry   2 hovercraft   3 cruise ship   4 yacht

A ☐   B ☐   C ☐   D ☐

2 Prediction

Discuss these predictions with a partner. Which do you think will happen?

1 The three women get a ferry to England.

2 The three women find something important in the hire car.

3 The three businessmen follow the three women.

CHAPTER TWO Galway to Dublin

'Don't worry… I'll be there… I love you, too,' said Shauna, the Irish girl. She was on the phone.

'Was that your fiancé?' asked Harminda when Shauna finished speaking.

'Yes,' she replied with a smile.

'And you're getting married on Christmas Eve. That's so romantic!'

'I know. Graeme is romantic,' she said. She took a photo from her purse and gave it to Harminda. It was obvious that she loved him very much. 'He even proposed on Valentine's Day'.

'Original,' said Vanessa sarcastically [1].

'What is your problem?' replied Shauna, angry at the blonde woman's sarcastic reply.

'I'm not the one with the problem. I'm not the one getting

---

1. **sarcastically** : said in a way to hurt another person.

married... thank God! We left Galway two hours ago and the only thing you've talked about is Gavin, and how wonderful he is.'

'His name's Graeme.'

'Graeme — Gavin — whatever. So he's romantic? After six months of marriage it won't be romantic, when you have to wash his dirty clothes every week!'

'Vanessa, that's a horrible thing to say!' said Harminda. 'Have you never been in love?'

For a moment, Vanessa's eyes went dark. 'Love is for idiots,' she said in a low voice.

Shauna touched the small diamond engagement ring on her left hand and looked out of the window; trying not to cry. She loved Graeme and he loved her, and on Christmas Eve she was going to marry him.

'Don't listen to her, Shauna!' said Harminda.

Shauna liked Harminda. She only looked about 22, but she seemed a lot older.

'At last!' thought Shauna when she saw a sign for Dublin Port.

But Harminda didn't slow down. She was arguing with Vanessa and she didn't see it.

'Harminda... the port... you've just missed the exit!' said Shauna.

'What? Are you sure?'

'Brilliant! This is all your fault!' [1] shouted Vanessa at Shauna.

'My fault! Why is it my fault?'

'Oh don't start all that again! I'll turn off at the next exit and we'll come back,' said Harminda.

But then the cars in front began to slow down and stop.

---

1. **This is all your fault** : This happened because of you.

'That's all we need... a traffic jam!' [1] said Vanessa. 'We'll never get there in time now!'

When they eventually [2] arrived at the ferry terminal, it was late. There were no cars or passengers waiting, only a security guard.

'Where do we go to get the ferry for Holyhead?' Shauna asked him.

The security guard pointed behind him at the ferry, which was already sailing away from the port.

'No...' they said at the same time.

'The next ferry is tomorrow morning, at ten to seven,' said the guard.

'This is all your fault!' shouted Vanessa.

'Oh, shut up!' Shauna and Harminda shouted back.

Luckily, they found a small hotel. They started to relax as they began to take their bags out of the car in the hotel garage.

'Don't forget your briefcase,' [3] Harminda said to Vanessa. She was pointing at a dark brown, expensive leather briefcase.

'It's not mine,' Vanessa said, pulling it from the car. It was quite heavy. 'Shauna, is it yours?'

'No.'

'And it's not mine,' said Harminda. 'So, it was already in the car when we left the airport. Somebody has obviously forgotten it.'

'What do you think is inside?' said Vanessa, and for the first time that day she smiled.

---

1. **traffic jam :** when there are a lot of cars, buses, etc., and they move very slowly.

2 **eventually :** in the end.

3. **briefcase :**

The text and **beyond**

1 Comprehension check

Are these sentences true (T) or false (F)? Correct the false ones.

	T	F
1 Shauna talks about Graeme a lot.	☐	☐
2 Vanessa believes in love.	☐	☐
3 Shauna doesn't like Harminda.	☐	☐
4 Harminda seems older than she looks.	☐	☐
5 The three women want to get a ferry from Dublin in Ireland to Holyhead in England.	☐	☐
6 They can't find a place for the night.	☐	☐
7 The briefcase was in the car before they hired it.	☐	☐
8 They open the briefcase in the hotel garage.	☐	☐

2 Question words

Complete the questions from Chapter Two below with the correct word from the box. There is one extra word.

> What (x 2)   Where   Who   Why

1 ....'s your problem?

2 .... do we go to get the ferry for Holyhead?

3 .... is it my fault?

4 .... do you think is inside?

Who asks these questions and what's the answer to them? Look back at Chapter Two to check.

3 With a partner, write four questions about Chapter Two using the question words in activity 2.

Example: **Student A:** Who's in love with a man called Graeme?

Student B: Shauna.

4 Characters

Now match the three characters to what they say.

A Harminda   **B** Vanessa   **C** Shauna

1 ☐ 'I love you, too.'

2 ☐ '...Graeme is romantic... He even proposed on Valentine's Day.'

3 ☐ 'I'm not the one with the problem. I'm not the one getting married... thank God!...'

4 ☐ '...So he's romantic? After six months of marriage it won't be romantic, when you have to wash his dirty clothes every week!'

5 ☐ 'Have you never been in love?'

6 ☐ 'Love is for idiots.'

5 Vocabulary – love and romance

Complete the sentences with the words/phrases from Chapter Two in the box. Put the verbs into the correct tense.

> engagement ring   fiancé   marriage   to be in love (with someone)
> to get married   to love (someone) (x2)
> to marry (someone)   to propose (to someone)

1 When he .... to me, I didn't say yes immediately. I wanted to think about it first.

2 Her .... is made of gold, with an enormous diamond.

3 .... isn't easy — being with the same person, day after day, year after year...

4 She's going to .... a man from Australia, and then they're going to live there.

5 He says he .... her, but I think he's too young to know what love really means.

6 They .... in the church in the village where her parents live. More than two hundred people came to the wedding.

7 He .... with her, but now she says that she .... another man. I don't know what they're going to do.

8 My .... doesn't want the wedding in a church, so it's going to be in a registry office.

6 **Listening**

track 05

Listen again to these two moments from Chapter Two:

'Original,' said Vanessa sarcastically.
'Brilliant! This is all your fault!' shouted Vanessa at Shauna.

Both 'original' and 'brilliant' are words that are normally used to show that we approve of something, but we can also say them in a way that shows the opposite meaning. This is called 'sarcasm'. When someone speaks sarcastically, he/she makes fun of someone, or even insults them.

Listen to the following sentences and phrases. Decide if the speaker is sarcastic or is showing approval. Underline or circle the word APPROVAL or SARCASM.

1   Thank you for your fascinating comment!   APPROVAL / SARCASM
2   That's a wonderful idea!   APPROVAL / SARCASM
3   Well, that was a great meal!   APPROVAL / SARCASM
4   Well, that was an interesting film!   APPROVAL / SARCASM
5   What a beautiful baby!   APPROVAL / SARCASM
6   What a lovely day!   APPROVAL / SARCASM
7   Oh, great!   APPROVAL / SARCASM
8   Don't worry about me — I'm fine!   APPROVAL / SARCASM

Now you say the sentences and phrases 1-8 above. First say them all in a way that shows approval, then say them all in a sarcastic way.

7 **Speaking**

In pairs or small groups, make up one or two very short conversations between two or three people. Include one of the sentences or phrases listed below in each of your conversations. Decide if the sentence or phrase shows approval or sarcasm. Then perform your conversation to the class.

- How romantic!
- It was such an interesting day!
- I can wait to see/read/listen to it!
- He/she is so generous!

The Emerald Isle

Ireland is sometimes called 'The Emerald Isle' [1] because a lot of the country is a beautiful green, like the colour of emeralds. [2] This is because it rains a lot in Ireland: in some places it even rains for 270 days a year. A small part of the north of the island, Northern Ireland, is a part of the United Kingdom. The rest of the island is the Republic of Ireland. It is called Eire in the Irish language.

County Galway is in the west, in the province of Connaught. The capital of County Galway is the old town of Galway. Many people in Galway are bilingual; they speak English but they also speak Irish. Galway is also famous for its oysters and the 'Claddagh'. [3]

1. **Isle** : island.
2. **emeralds** : green-coloured precious stones.
3. **Claddagh** : pronunciation klædə.

↓ Typical fishing boats in **Galway Harbour**.

A view over Galway Bay towards Galway. The photo is taken from one of the three **Aran Islands**.

The Claddagh is a ring named after a fishing village near Galway where they first made it. It shows a heart with a crown on it, with two hands holding the heart. The hands mean friendship, the crown means loyalty and the heart means love. Tradition says that if you wear the ring on your left hand, with the crown pointing outward and the heart pointing towards your hand, it means you are married. If you wear the ring on your right hand in the same way (with the crown pointing outward and the heart pointing towards your hand) it is like an engagement ring: it means you are going out with someone. But if you wear the ring on your right hand, with the crown pointing inward and the heart pointing away from your hand, it means you are free.

Off the west coast are the beautiful Aran Islands. These are famous for the traditional style of life of the people who live there, and for the woollen pullovers which they make by hand.

200 kilometres to the east of Galway is Dublin, the capital of Ireland. It was once a poor city, but today, after the economic boom of the 1980s and 1990s, it is one of the most exciting cities in Europe.

The O'Connell Bridge across the **River Liffey in Dublin**. The O'Connell Bridge, built in 1794-98, is the second oldest of Dublin's eleven bridges.

Dublin is more famous for its people than for historical buildings. People say that Dubliners, and Irish people in general, are very relaxed and have a sense of humour. And they love 'craic' (pronounced 'crack'), the Irish word for 'having a good time'.

Trinity College, Ireland's most important university, is to the south of the River Liffey. Famous writers who have studied at Trinity College include Jonathan Swift, the author of *Gulliver's Travels*, Bram Stoker, the author of *Dracula*, and Oscar Wilde, the author of *The Importance of Being Earnest*.

But Dublin's most famous writer is James Joyce. In his novel *Ulysses* (1922), Joyce wrote about what happened to a group of people during just one day in Dublin: 16 June 1904. Now, every year on 16 June, Dubliners celebrate 'Bloomsday' by visiting places from the novel and wearing clothes that people wore in 1904.

Another important date for Irish people is 17 March, Saint Patrick's Day. Saint Patrick is the patron saint of Ireland. On this date, Irish people all over the world celebrate this festival with lots of Irish songs and music, and by drinking Ireland's most famous beer, Guinness.

1 Factfile

Fill in this factfile about Ireland.

Capital	....
Weather	....
Traditional products	....
Food and drink	....
Famous university	....
Famous writers	....
Names & date of festival(s)	....
Other interesting fact(s)	....

2 Make a factfile, in English, about your own country.

 INTERNET PROJECT

Connect to the Internet and go to www.blackcat-cideb.com or www.cideb.it . Insert the title or part of the title of the book into our search engine. Open the page for *Home for Christmas*. Click on the Internet project link. Go down the page until you find the title of this book and click on the link for this project.

▶ Because of Ireland's history, there are many Irish people all over the world. In the first website, find out how many places in the world celebrate Saint Patrick's Day in a big way. Are you surprised?

▶ The second website is about the celebrations in Dublin. Take the quick tour, and download the pictures that interest you most. Describe them to the class.

Before you read

1 **Vocabulary**

Match the following words to the correct picture below.

A blanket   **B** clip   **C** lock   **D** label   **E** tear   **F** sunglasses

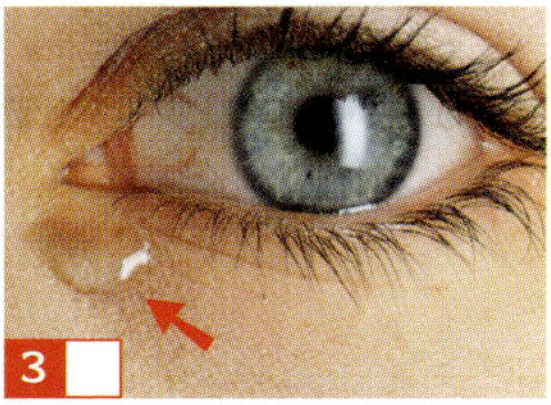

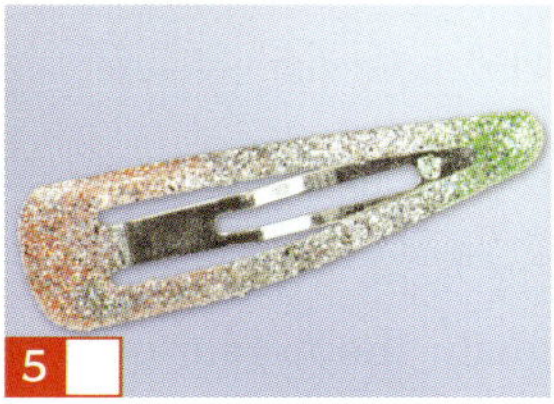

2 Now complete these sentences with a word from activity 1.

1 It was a very cold night so Fergal got an extra .... to keep him warm.

2 Angela's hair was too long so she used a .... to hold it in place.

3 They tried to open the cupboard to see what was inside but they needed a key to open the ....

4 I'm on a diet so I always read the .... before buying any food to see the calories.

5 There were .... in Jim's eyes when his dog was hurt by a car.

6 Brendan needs to wear .... when he's driving in sunny weather.

3 **Prediction**

Look at these two sentences from Chapter Three:

... Slowly she opened the briefcase. Her eyes became big and round when she saw what was inside.

Who do you think opens the briefcase? What do think is inside it? Talk about it in pairs, then tell the class.

CHAPTER **THREE** **A Sleepless Night**

'**I want to open it!**' said Vanessa.

'But it's not ours,' said Harminda. It was one o'clock in the morning and she was in bed, trying to sleep. 'We've got to be up in less than four hours if we want to get the first ferry. So please... Go to sleep!' Vanessa turned away from the briefcase and pulled the blanket over her head.

'We couldn't open it anyway. It's locked,' said Shauna, getting into bed. But then she noticed Vanessa's smile. 'What? Why are you smiling?'

Vanessa took a clip from her hair and held it between her fingers.

'That'll never work,' laughed Shauna.

'It always works in films.'

'Go on then!' said Shauna, 'Do it!'

Harminda pulled the blankets over her head.

Vanessa worked on one of the locks, using her clip as a key.

'I knew it,' said Shauna after a few minutes, 'I didn't think it was going to work...' but before she could finish her sentence there was a click and the lock opened.

Harminda sat up in bed. This didn't seem the right thing to do. But now it was open, she wanted to know what was inside.

Vanessa soon opened the other lock... Slowly she opened the briefcase. Her eyes became big and round when she saw what was inside.

Harminda watched their shocked faces, 'What's in it? Show me!'

Vanessa turned the case towards her.

The briefcase was full of money.

After a few moments, Harminda said, 'There are hundreds of thousands of euros here!' She laughed nervously, 'I've never seen so much money! There's only one thing we can do now.'

'What are you doing?' Vanessa said when she saw Harminda with her mobile phone in her hand.

'I'm going to phone the police.'

'You can't do that! Do you realise what a difference this money could make to my... to our lives!'

'But it's not ours!'

'We don't know whose it is. There's no label, no name... Tell her, Shauna!'

'Shauna... you know we have to go to the police, don't you?' said Harminda.

'I don't know... my fiancé and I really want a honeymoon. [1] We could go anywhere in the world with this money: the Maldives, the Caribbean, New York, San Francisco... anywhere. At the moment we're going to stay in my parents' caravan.' [2] Shauna looked into Harminda's

---

1. **honeymoon :** a holiday after you get married.   2. **caravan :**

eyes. 'We've never had a holiday together... I'm sorry, Harminda.'

Vanessa held Harminda's hands. Her voice was soft and kind and Harminda remembered that she was an actress. 'You said your Dad's ill. Think about it. With this money, you could pay for the best doctors...'

Harminda's phone started to ring. Slowly Harminda picked it up and answered. 'Hello... oh, hello Mum. How's Dad?'

When the phone call finished ten minutes later, her cheeks [1] were wet with tears.

'What is it Harminda?' asked Shauna.

'My Dad... He's got worse. They're not sure if he will survive...'

Vanessa closed the briefcase. 'Well then, you need to get there quickly. If we go to the police now, they'll ask us questions for hours...'

'OK,' said Harminda quietly.

'Maybe not until tomorrow,' continued Vanessa.

'I said OK! We won't go to the police now, but when we get to London, after I've seen my Dad, then we'll go. Do you all agree?'

Shauna nodded [2] reluctantly, but Vanessa only said, 'Let's get a few hours' sleep now. We don't want to miss the next ferry.'

This time they arrived early and waited in the car. It wasn't snowing, but it was cold and everything looked very dark.

When they started to drive onto the ferry, Harminda saw the face of the driver of the car behind her. 'That's strange,' she thought. 'It's still dark outside but he's wearing sunglasses.'

'Are you OK?' asked Shauna.

'I'm... cold... that's all.' Harminda answered. But she didn't seem sure of what she was saying.

---

1. **cheeks :** the soft parts of your face below your eyes.
2. **nodded :** moved her head up and down to say 'yes'.

The text and **beyond**

KET 1 Comprehension check

Are these sentences 'Right' (A) or 'Wrong' (B)? If there is not enough information to answer 'Right' or 'Wrong' choose 'Doesn't say' (C). There is an example at the beginning (0).

0 The briefcase is not easy to open.
  (A) Right   **B** Wrong   **C** Doesn't say

1 Shauna says Vanessa must not open the briefcase.
  A Right   **B** Wrong   **C** Doesn't say

2 Harminda calls the police.
  A Right   **B** Wrong   **C** Doesn't say

3 Shauna thinks it's a good idea to call the police.
  A Right   **B** Wrong   **C** Doesn't say

4 Harminda discovers that her father may die.
  A Right   **B** Wrong   **C** Doesn't say

5 They decide to go to the police later.
  A Right   **B** Wrong   **C** Doesn't say

6 The man in the car behind is following them.
  A Right   **B** Wrong   **C** Doesn't say

2 Listening

Listen and match the characters from Chapter Three to what they say.

A Harminda   **B** Vanessa   **C** Shauna

Audio	1	2	3	4	5	6	7
Character							

3 Vocabulary – verbs and adjectives plus prepositions

Complete the phrases from Chapter Three with the correct preposition from the box.

of   on   for (x2)   to   into

1 get .... bed
2 full .... money
3 pay .... her ticket

4 concentrate .... the lock
5 reach .... her mobile phone
6 get .... London

4 **Fill in the gaps**

Complete the text below with phrases from activity 2. There is an example at the beginning (0).

Delia was in a hurry to (0) get to work.. because she had an important meeting. The streets were (1)........................ traffic and people but she was (2) .... finding a free taxi. Eventually, she found one and (3) .... it. She told the taxi driver where to go and ten minutes later they arrived at her office. She (4) .... her purse but it wasn't there! 'Oh no!' she cried. 'Someone has stolen my purse!'

5 **Discussion**

Ask and answer the following questions about Chapter Three with a partner.

1 Was Vanessa wrong to open the briefcase?
2 Should Harminda go to the police?
3 Vanessa says the money could help Harminda's father. Do you believe that Vanessa really cares about this?
4 Why does Shauna tell Vanessa to open the case?
5 Is it dangerous not to go to the police?
6 Who is the man wearing sunglasses?
7 Which of the three female characters do you think is the most interesting? Why?

6 **The euro**

In the briefcase there are hundreds of thousands of euros. The euro is the currency of many European countries; the word 'currency' means the money that is used in a country. Talk about the questions first — can you answer them? Then read the passage to find out the answers.

1 How many countries use the euro?
2 Are there countries in the European Union that don't use the euro?
3 When did European countries start using the euro?
4 What were the names of some national currencies before the euro?
5 Do all the countries use the same words for the euro currency?
6 Are all euro coins and notes the same?

The euro (the symbol is €) is the official currency of the Eurozone, also called the Euro Area: it includes Austria, Belgium, Finland, France, Germany, Greece, Ireland, Italy, Luxembourg, the Netherlands, Portugal, Slovenia, and Spain. From 1 January 2008, Cyprus and Malta are included too. All member states of the  European Union (EU) can use the euro if they want – and if they follow some rules – but not all EU members want to use the currency at the moment: the United Kingdom, Denmark and Sweden use their own currency. Some very small European states – the Vatican, Monaco and San Marino – are not EU members but they use the euro because their currency is connected to other EU members. Other states – Andorra, Montenegro and Kosovo – use the euro even if they haven't got a legal connection with the EU yet.

The currency was introduced in banking at midnight on 1 January 1999. The notes and coins of the old currencies continued to be used, however, until the first euro coins and banknotes came out on 1 January 2002. Some of the currencies used before were the Austrian schilling, the Belgian and French francs, the German mark, the Greek drachma, the Irish pound, the Italian lira, the Portuguese escudo and the Spanish peseta. On 1 January 2007 Slovenia changed its tolar for the euro.

The euro is divided into 100 cents, except in Greece, which uses λεπτό (lepto, singular) and λεπτά (lepta, plural) instead of cents. On all euro coins the side that shows the value is the same everywhere in the Eurozone, but the other side has an image that the individual states choose. All euro banknotes are the same on both sides: the theme is European architecture in various artistic periods. The front of the notes shows windows, arches or gates while the back shows bridges: the symbolic message is about being open and being connected. The architectural examples shown, however, do not represent real, existing monuments, so that countries do not argue about what monuments to choose for the notes.

Before you read

1 Prediction

Harminda last saw her parents four years ago. Why such a long time ago, do you think? Share your ideas, then read and find out.

CHAPTER **FOUR** # On the Ferry

It was dawn [1] **and Shauna and Harminda looked at the red and orange sky over Dublin as the ferry slowly left the port.**

track 08

'When was the last time you saw your parents?' Shauna asked Harminda.

'Four years ago… At my eighteenth birthday party,' she answered sadly.

'Wow… That's a long time.'

'They wanted me to marry someone else… Somebody they chose.'

'An arranged marriage?' [2]

'Yes,' said Harminda.

They stood in silence for a while.

'In Indian tradition, a marriage is more than just a woman and a man being together. It's a marriage of two families. I've always

---

1. **dawn :** early morning, when the sun comes up.
2. **arranged marriage :** in this kind of marriage the parents choose who their son or daughter will marry.

known that it was very important to my family. But then I met Declan. I was only 17, but I knew that I wanted to spend the rest of my life with him. We saw each other in secret for months. I was too frightened to tell my family about it, because they believe in arranged marriages. But then my parents told me the big news: at my eighteenth birthday party they wanted to introduce me to my future husband, an Indian boy. I knew that I had to tell them the truth. I'm the only daughter — I've just got one brother — and my father was very angry. I had to choose, he told me... And I chose Declan.'

'Are you still together?'

'Yes,' said Harminda, and she touched her stomach.

'Are you pregnant?' [1] Shauna asked with a smile.

'Yes, I only got the news last week.' She laughed, 'You're the only other person that knows. I haven't told Declan yet!'

'I'm sure that when your Dad knows he'll be happy too!'

'Maybe...'

Three hours later, they were in England.

Harminda drove fast; they had to drive for another six hours before they arrived in London.

After a few miles, Harminda noticed that Vanessa was looking over her shoulder.

'What's wrong, Vanessa?'

'I... Nothing...' she said. 'Can't you drive faster?'

'I'm already driving over the speed limit. Why?'

'No reason, it's only... I don't want to frighten anyone... but I think somebody is following us. There's a dark blue car behind us. It's been there since we got on the ferry at Dublin.'

---

1. **pregnant** : going to have a baby.

Harminda looked in the mirror. Her heart began to beat faster when she saw the sunglasses.

Suddenly, they heard a horn. [1] Harminda looked back at the road and saw that an enormous lorry was coming directly towards them.

She turned the steering wheel to the right and pushed her foot down hard on the brake. [2] But the lorry was getting nearer.

1. **horn** : on a vehicle such as a car, the horn is the device that makes a loud noise as a signal or warning.
2. **brake** : this stops a car.

The car seemed out of control.

Someone screamed. [1]

But then the lorry passed by them. The car slowed down and Harminda's body relaxed.

Suddenly there was a loud noise.

The three women all turned around.

They saw the lorry crashing into the car that was following them.

1. **screamed** : made a loud, high noise with the voice.

The text and **beyond**

KET **1** **Comprehension check**

Choose the correct answer — A, B or C.

1 When Harminda was eighteen her family wanted her
  - **A** ☐ to go and live in Ireland.
  - **B** ☐ to marry someone they chose for her.
  - **C** ☐ to marry her boyfriend Declan.

2 Harminda made a decision which made her father
  - **A** ☐ happy.
  - **B** ☐ proud.
  - **C** ☐ angry.

3 The only person who knows that Harminda is pregnant is
  - **A** ☐ Vanessa.
  - **B** ☐ Declan.
  - **C** ☐ Shauna.

4 Vanessa is nervous because
  - **A** ☐ she sees the man with sunglasses following them.
  - **B** ☐ Harminda is driving too fast.
  - **C** ☐ they will arrive in London late.

5 There is a crash between
  - **A** ☐ a lorry and the car with the three women.
  - **B** ☐ a lorry and the blue car.
  - **C** ☐ the blue car and the car with the three women.

2 **Vocabulary – irregular verbs in the past simple tense**

Complete these sentences from Chapter Four with the correct form. The infinitives of each verb are in the box.

| meet   have to   know   get   see (x2)   choose   tell |

1 When was the last time you .... your parents?
2 Then I .... Declan. I was only 17.
3 I .... that I wanted to spend the rest of my life with him.
4 We .... each other in secret for months.
5 But then my parents .... me the big news.

6   I .... choose, he told me.

7   And I .... Declan.

8   I only .... the news last week.

③ Fill in the gaps

Complete this newspaper article about an arranged marriage with the correct form of an irregular verb from the previous activity.

Sanjay and his parents are Indians who live in England and believe in the traditional customs of India. When Sanjay was twenty-five, his parents **(1)** .... someone to be his wife — a pretty, eighteen-year-old Indian girl called Rita. When Sanjay **(2)**......................... Rita, he liked her, and **(3)**......................... his parents he was happy to marry her. They got married a few weeks later. At the start of their marriage they had problems, but they **(4)**......................... that, if they wanted to make their marriage work , they **(5)**......................... be honest and patient with each other.

④ Discussion

Now ask and answer the following questions with a partner.

1   At what age do people normally get married in your country?

2   What reasons do people usually have for wanting to get married?

3   How do you think your parents' choice of a marriage partner for you would be different from your own choice?

4   Decide on three possible reasons in favour of arranged marriage and three reasons against.

KET ⑤ Weddings

Read the article about British weddings. Choose the best word(s) — A, B or C — for each space. The first one is done as an example (0).

The ceremony at which people get married is **(0)** ..C.. a wedding. A wedding in which people get married **(1)** .... the 'eyes of the law' is called a civil marriage, but most religions also organise weddings, **(2)** .... that people can be married in the 'eyes of God'. In the United States, the United Kingdom and the Republic of Ireland, both kinds of ceremonies can take place **(3)** .... the same time; the priest at the religious ceremony **(4)** .... the people who are getting married to sign an official register: if this does not happen the marriage is not legal. In most countries weddings take place (**5**) .... in a 'registry office', for civil marriages without any religious ceremony, or in a church. In some countries however, such as the United Kingdom and Australia, marriages can take place in private and in (**6**) .... place.

At weddings you can see many examples of national traditions: here are (**7**) .... elements of a traditional British wedding. The woman (**8**) .... takes part in the ceremony is called the 'bride' and the man is called the 'bridegroom' or 'groom'; after the ceremony they become a wife and a husband. They arrive separately (**9**) .... the place of the wedding: with the groom is a close friend called the 'best man'; with the bride are female friends and family members called 'bridesmaids'. The (**10**) .... important part of the wedding is when the bride and groom make their 'vows' — these are serious promises to love each (**11**) .... and look after each other — and give rings to each other.

Some elements of the traditional ceremony show that the bride (**12**) .... her father's family and goes to a new family with her husband; for example, during the wedding the bride's father 'gives away' the (**13**) .... Nowadays, such elements are simply traditional: a husband and wife now have the same rights and social position. After the wedding there is an event with food and drink called a 'reception'. It is traditional (**14**) .... the best man and the father of the bride to give speeches, when they stand (**15**) .... and talk — often in an amusing way — (**16**) .... the groom and bride when they were younger. Often there is music and dancing, too. After the reception the couple (**17**) .... on a holiday called a 'honeymoon': this sixteenth-century word (**18**) .... the idea that the first month of the marriage is the sweetest!

0	**A** known	**B** named	**C** called
1	**A** for	**B** under	**C** in
2	**A** in	**B** so	**C** for
3	**A** in	**B** at	**C** on
4	**A** asks	**B** asks for	**C** asks to
5	**A** either	**B** or	**C** both
6	**A** some	**B** every	**C** any
7	**A** few	**B** some	**C** all
8	**A** who	**B** that	**C** which
9	**A** at	**B** in	**C** to

10	**A** main	**B** more	**C** most
11	**A** one	**B** other	**C** them
12	**A** departs	**B** goes away	**C** leaves
13	**A** wife	**B** groom	**C** bride
14	**A** that	**B** for	**C** when
15	**A** up	**B** well	**C** formally
16	**A** regard	**B** to	**C** about
17	**A** go away	**B** go out	**C** go home
18	**A** is by	**B** comes from	**C** derives

6 Speaking

Describe marriages in your country or region to a visitor. Explain how people there usually get married nowadays, and what the traditional wedding customs are. You can also compare and contrast the customs with those in the UK. In your description, include:

- religious and civil weddings
- places you can get married
- what the bride and groom wear (the photo shows a British wedding)
- most important part(s) of the wedding
- importance of family and friends
- what happens after the wedding

Before you read

1 Prediction

Discuss these predictions with a partner. Which do you think will happen?

1   The three women are killed in a car accident.
2   The three women are attacked by the people following them.
3   We discover something about Vanessa's past.
4   A character from an earlier chapter is killed.
5   The women tell the police about the money.

CHAPTER **FIVE** # The Road to London

They drove the rest of the journey in silence.

Three hours later, when they stopped to get petrol, [1] they were still nervous.

'I need to get some air,' Vanessa said, getting out of the car. 'Are you coming, too, Shauna?'

Shauna shook her head.

Vanessa didn't want to go anywhere by herself. She turned to Harminda.

'What about you?' she asked.

'I want to leave as soon as I've filled the car up with petrol,' said Harminda.

Vanessa felt stupid for being so nervous, but she couldn't stop herself.

---

1. **petrol :** a liquid put into cars to make them move.

In the toilets she looked at herself in the mirror and laughed. She looked terrible. Without make-up she looked older than thirty-five.

But she was alive.

When Ben left her for her best friend, she was only twenty-five with the lead role ¹ in a musical ² that was going to take her all over the world. But she gave it all up ³ because she loved him and she didn't want to be away from him.

In the end, he left her anyway.

There were other boyfriends, but for the last ten years she never really loved anyone else because she never wanted to be hurt again. She was never afraid of anything, because there was nothing left to lose... until today.

Now, after the crash, things were different. Vanessa wanted to live. She wanted to change.

Why didn't she listen to Harminda? Why didn't they go to the police before? Now it was too late. Why did she never listen?

She went inside and ordered a cup of coffee.

The person behind the bar was reading a newspaper. Vanessa saw the date: 22 December. They only left Galway yesterday. It seemed a lot longer.

There was a small television on the wall over the bar. The news was on.

'... A body was found in the car park of Galway Airport, Ireland, in the early hours of this morning. Thirty-three-year-old Colin O'Flaherty, manager of a car hire at Galway Airport, was

---

1. **lead role :** the most important part.
2. **musical :** a show at the theatre with singing and dancing.
3. **gave it all up:** decided not to do it.

shot [1] in the chest. The police believe the killing was related to drug trafficking...' [2]

'It's terrible, isn't it?' said the barman, passing Vanessa her glass of water. Vanessa realised that she was staring at the television. Her face was white, her mouth open. 'It's in the newspapers... look...' He passed her the newspaper.

'FAMILY MAN KILLED IN DRUGS SHOOTING' said the headline. In the centre of the page there was a photo of Colin O'Flaherty on holiday with his three-year-old son. They were obviously on a boat and Colin was holding a very big fish. They looked so happy.

Vanessa felt sick.

She looked back at the television; a young woman was crying. At the bottom of the screen, Vanessa read, 'Mrs Moira O'Flaherty, Mr O'Flaherty's wife.'

'If anyone knows anything, anything at all... please — for my little boy — please contact the police.' Her voice sounded more and more desperate. Vanessa felt like the woman was talking directly to her.

'Anything at all... please...'

Vanessa couldn't hear any more. She ran from the bar, still holding the newspaper in her left hand.

1. **shot :** hit with a bullet fired out of a gun.
2. **drug trafficking :** buying and selling of drugs.

The text and **beyond**

1 Comprehension check

Are these sentences true (T) or false (F)? Correct the false ones.

		T	F
1	The three women feel much better.	☐	☐
2	They all go into the bar together.	☐	☐
3	Vanessa has had a bad experience in a relationship in the past.	☐	☐
4	Vanessa is sorry that she didn't listen to Harminda before.	☐	☐
5	Vanessa discovers that the manager from the car hire office at Galway Airport is dead.	☐	☐
6	Vanessa contacts the police after hearing Mr O'Flaherty's wife on the television.	☐	☐

2 Time expressions

Complete the sentences below from Chapter Five with the correct time expression.

> **as soon as   in the end   later   until**

1 Three hours ...., when they stopped to get petrol, they were still nervous.

2 'I want to leave .... I've filled the car up with petrol,' said Harminda.

3 ...., he left her anyway.

4 She was never afraid of anything, because there was nothing left to lose .... today.

Now match each of the time expressions above with its definition.

A after   ....

B finally   ....

C immediately after   ....

D not before this time ....

3 Characters

Vanessa asks herself the following questions. Put the words in the correct order.

1 didn't / Harminda? / listen / she / to / Why
2 before? / didn't / go / police / the / they / to / Why
3 did / listen? / never / she / Why

Now, with a partner, try and answer the questions.

4 Vocabulary – crime

Match each of the following crimes with one of the definitions below.

A drug dealing C kidnapping E burglary
B murder D bank robbery F hit-and-run

1 ☐ using or threatening violence to steal money from a bank
2 ☐ entering a building by force and stealing things
3 ☐ hitting someone with your car and driving away without stopping
4 ☐ deliberate and illegal killing of a person
5 ☐ buying and selling of illegal substances
6 ☐ taking someone by force and demanding money to set them free

5 Listening

track 10

Listen to the news reports and match each one with a crime from activity 4. Two crimes are not mentioned.

Speaker	1	2	3	4
Crime				

6 Vocabulary – look/sound + adjective

Which character(s) from Chapter Five is/are each of the following sentences about?

A She looked terrible. ....
B Without make-up she looked older than thirty-five. ....
C They looked so happy. ....
D Her voice sounded more and more desperate. ....

Now complete the following sentences with *look* or *sound*. Use the correct tense.

1 You .... exhausted! Your eyes are red. Didn't you sleep last night?
2 They .... so happy in their wedding photos. I can't believe they're going to get divorced.
3 She .... terrible when I phoned her this morning.
4 Your face is very white. You .... well. Can I get you an aspirin?
5 Are you sure you're OK? From your voice, you .... really depressed. What's the matter?

Before you read

1 Prediction

Harminda is going to meet her family again, after four years. What do you think will happen in Chapter Six? Harminda is going to meet her family, after four years. What do you think will happen in Chapter Six? Discuss these questions with a partner.

Harminda's mother.
1 What do you think her mother's reaction will be when she sees Harminda again?
2 Do you think she will get as angry as Harminda's father?
3 Will she try and make Harminda's father change his mind about Declan?

Harminda's father.
4 Will he still be very angry with Harminda even if he is ill?
5 Do you think Harminda will make him change his mind? How?
6 Will he survive?

Harminda's brother.
7 Will he be surprised when he sees Harminda?
8 Will he speak in favour of his father's idea of marriage?
9 Will he try to convince his father to speak to Harminda again?

CHAPTER SIX At the Hospital

track 11

'Go on. We'll wait here for you,' said Shauna.

'But what if they come back?'

'You saw that accident. We'll be alright for a couple of hours,' insisted Vanessa.

Harminda looked nervously at the hospital. She took a deep breath and got out of the car. 'I'll be as quick as I can, but this is my mobile number, if you need me.'

She quickly wrote it down and gave it to Shauna.

Inside the hospital, Harminda took the lift to the ninth floor.

When the doors opened, her little brother was waiting for her. But he wasn't so little any more. The last time she saw him he was nine years old, a child. Now he was thirteen and he was a lot taller than Harminda. There were so many things she wanted to ask him, but she could only say his name: 'Parindra?'

'What is she doing here?' her father's voice interrupted them. He was seriously ill but his voice was still strong.

49

'Meena? Did you ask her to come here?'

Meena, Harminda's mother, looked elegant in a red silk sari. When she saw her daughter there were tears of happiness in her eyes.

'Dad? Oh Dad, I've missed you so much!' Harminda ran towards him. His face was grey, his hair was thinner than she remembered, and he looked old and weak. But his eyes were angry. Just like they were four years ago.

'I don't want you here. You made your decision. Please leave!'

Harminda touched his hand but he closed his eyes and turned away from her.

'But I've come from Ireland! Dad, please listen to me... Dad!' she shouted as they took him into the operating room on a trolley, Meena and Parindra next to him.

'I love you, Dad,' she said, but he was gone.

She was alone in the long, white corridor.

She sat down, put her head in her hands and cried. All her hopes of a happy reunion were gone.

It was not going to be easy for him to meet her again — Harminda knew that. But she didn't think it was going to be this difficult.

Why didn't he understand that she never wanted to choose? Why couldn't he see that she was still his daughter, still his little girl? Why couldn't he see that she still needed her Dad? Even if she loved Declan.

When she couldn't cry any more, she stood up and decided to go with Shauna and Vanessa to the police station.

'Later on, I'll come back. And I won't leave until he understands,' she thought as she went outside.

When she got to the car park the car was there, but there was no Shauna and Vanessa... And there was no briefcase full of money.

The text and **beyond**

KET **①** **Comprehension check**

Are these sentences 'Right' (A) or 'Wrong' (B)? If there is not enough information to answer 'Right' or 'Wrong' choose 'Doesn't say' (C). There is an example at the beginning (0).

0 Vanessa and Shauna wait for two hours in the car park.
   A Right   **B** Wrong   **C** Doesn't say

1 Harminda gives Shauna the number of her mobile phone.
   A Right   **B** Wrong   **C** Doesn't say

2 Harminda's father is called Parindra.
   A Right   **B** Wrong   **C** Doesn't say

3 Harminda's father has forgiven her.
   A Right   **B** Wrong   **C** Doesn't say

4 Harminda's mother is happy to see her.
   A Right   **B** Wrong   **C** Doesn't say

5 Harminda thinks that her father will change his mind about her soon.
   A Right   **B** Wrong   **C** Doesn't say

6 When Harminda gets back to the car park, Vanessa and Shauna aren't there.
   A Right   **B** Wrong   **C** Doesn't say

② **Characters**

Answer these questions about the characters in Chapter Six.

Who

1 is a tall teenager?

2 doesn't have much hair?

3 is wearing traditional Indian clothes?

4 looks angry?

5 cries when he/she sees someone in her/his family?

6 cries because of the attitude of someone in her/his family?

3 **Discussion**

Complete the following sentences from Chapter Six.

1   Harminda: 'Dad? Oh Dad, I've .... you so much!'
2   Harminda's father: 'I don't .... you here. You made your ....'

Now discuss these questions with a partner.

• Did Harminda make the right decision when she left her family to go to Ireland with Declan? Why/Why not?

• Is her father right when he doesn't forgive her? Why/Why not?

• Can young people make their own decisions about important events in their lives? Or is it better if their families decide for them? Give reasons for your decision.

Before you read

1 **Prediction**

Discuss these predictions with a partner. Which do you think will happen?

1   Shauna and Vanessa go away with the money.
2   The three men (from the first chapter) take Shauna and Vanessa with them.
3   One of the women is killed or badly hurt.
4   Harminda doesn't know what has happened to Shauna and Vanessa.
5   There is another car crash.
6   The police catch the three men.

Young Indian women shopping in London. They are wearing trousers, scarves and the **traditional sari**.

Indians in Britain

Introduction

Indians are Britain's largest ethnic minority: about 23% of the total ethnic population - people from Asia, China, the Caribbean, etc. – are Indian.

In the nineteenth century, India was part of the British Empire and Indians could enter the UK because they were British subjects.

But the majority of Indians began to immigrate to Britain in the 1950s and 1960s. Many found jobs in factories, especially factories making clothes. They planned to spend a maximum of ten years to earn enough money to go back home. But when they found jobs and a place to live, their families could come and stay with them. As a result, many Indians stayed in Britain; large numbers made their homes in areas such as Bradford in the north of England, Leicester and Birmingham in central England, and parts of London.

By 1961, more than 100,000 people of Indian and Pakistani nationality were resident in Britain.

A taste of home

Of course, moving to a different country was not easy. Many Indians left behind large families and, at first, they were lonely in Britain.

But gradually the British-Indian community grew bigger and bigger. They opened specialist shops where people could buy Indian food. They could then cook traditional dishes which reminded them of home. Today, curry has become part of British cuisine: some people even say that 'chicken tikka masala' is the most popular dish in Britain.

Popular culture

Ravi Shankar, a famous sitar [1] player and father of the singer Norah Jones, helped introduce Indian music to the western world in the 1960s when he taught Indian music to the Beatles. Recently, British Asians have developed 'Bhangra' music, which has become popular in the United Kingdom. This music combines western disco and reggae music with Indian folk music.

Indian culture can now be found in British television programmes and films, like the 2002 hit *Bend It Like Beckham*.

In the 1950s and 1960s life was hard for Asians in Britain: they were treated badly by some white people. But they brought different tastes, music and traditions with them and today, although there are still some problems, Asian communities play an important part in the multicultural society of Britain.

1. **sitar :**

Dancers celebrating **Diwali** in Trafalgar Square, London. Diwali has become one of London's major festivals.

Festivals

Diwali, 'The Festival of Lights', is the most popular Hindu festival. Diwali is celebrated on the night of the new moon in the month of Katrika in the Hindu Vikrama calendar. This is usually in October or November and the festival lasts five days.

It is a New Year festival that celebrates the victory of good over evil, light over darkness and knowledge over ignorance.

It is known as the festival of lights because people decorate their homes with lights. They place lamps called 'diyas' in windows and doors which are left open, so that Lakshmi, the goddess of wealth, can come into people's homes.

As well as decorating buildings with lights, Hindus celebrate Diwali in other ways: they give each other presents, they clean their homes, they wear new clothes and they have firework displays.

① Comprehension check

Answer the following questions.

1 Why could Indians enter Britain in the nineteenth century?
2 Why did many Indians enter Britain in the middle of the twentieth century?
3 What is curry?
4 What is the impact of Asian culture on contemporary Britain?

② Discussion

What is the biggest ethnic minority group in your country? When and why did they start arriving? What is their cultural impact?

 INTERNET PROJECT

Connect to the Internet and go to www.blackcat-cideb.com or www.cideb.it . Insert the title or part of the title of the book into our search engine. Open the page for *Home for Christmas*. Click on the Internet project link. Go down the page until you find the title of this book and click on the link for this project.

On page 55 you found out something about Diwali. Now let's find out some more. Go to the first website and find out

▶ what the name Diwali comes from, and what it means,
▶ what presents people give each other,
▶ what two important legends explain the beginning of Diwali.

Go to the second website, which is the BBC's dedicated website for Asians in Britain.

▶ Look at the homepage. How much of it seems to be about music?
▶ Follow the link to the soap opera, 'Silver Street'. Find out more about the characters. How many of the families are Asian? What ethnicity are the other families?

CHAPTER **SEVEN** # Danger Money

Shauna and Vanessa were in the back of the car. Their hands were tied. [1] They were very frightened as they tried to listen to the conversation of the two men in front of them.

'What are you going to do with your ten per cent of the money, Steve?'

'I'd like to go on a nice holiday, somewhere hot. What about you?'

Vanessa looked at the two men. She had to concentrate, she had to think of a plan. And she needed to think quickly. But she could only think of one thing: Colin O'Flaherty's three-year-old son.

While they were waiting for Harminda outside the hospital, these two men came up to them. They were smiling and seemed nice when they asked for directions to King's Cross station. But when Shauna was pointing the best way to them, the two men pushed them both into their car.

1. **tied :**

They wanted the briefcase.

'Did you see that crash between the lorry and the car with the plain-clothes [1] police?' laughed Steve.

He saw the way Vanessa and Shauna looked at each other, suddenly realising the truth.

'Did you think that was us?' laughed the driver. 'They thought that was us in that accident!' and they laughed even louder.

Just then their telephone rang. The driver answered the call, 'Yes, boss... OK... the old building in East London... of course we've got the money; we're not stupid... and the two ladies... no there were only two... what do you mean, there's another one? You'll have to go and get her!'

Vanessa knew then what she had to do.

Carefully, she pulled her mobile phone from her coat pocket and started to write a text message:

U R IN DANGER. MEN TAKING US 2 BUILDING IN EAST LONDON. B CAREFUL. MAN COMING 4 U. GO 2 POLICE. S&V

It seemed to take forever to write the short message. She took out the piece of paper with Harminda's number on it and typed: 354 781 2330.

Now, she only needed to press 'SEND' and then Harminda could get help.

'Hey! What are you doing! Give me that...!' Steve turned around and tried to grab [2] the phone.

Vanessa tried to press 'SEND', but he was pulling the phone out of her hand.

---

1. **plain-clothes** : wearing ordinary clothes, not in police uniform.
2. **grab** : take quickly.

'Leave her alone!' shouted Shauna, pulling on his arm, trying to free Vanessa.

The driver was looking at them, and couldn't control the car any more.

Steve got out his gun but Shauna pushed him and he dropped it.

'You stupid woman!' he shouted as he looked desperately around his feet for it.

Just then, a police siren [1] sounded in the distance. Steve looked up and saw that a police car was blocking the road in front of them. Its blue light was bright in the dark evening.

The driver pushed his foot down hard on the brake.

Shauna realised with horror that they were going straight for it... too fast!

The car began to move from side to side, dangerously out of control.

Vanessa screamed.

Shauna held her breath, [2] ready for the crash. She closed her eyes, waiting. Her body went quickly forwards, and then back. But there was no crash.

When she was sure that the car wasn't moving any more, she slowly opened her eyes.

The car was just a few centimetres from a police car.

Suddenly, a lot of policemen were all around the car and Shauna could finally breathe.

Their nightmare [3] was over.

---

1. **siren :** the noise a police car makes when there is an emergency.
2. **held her breath :** she didn't let air come into and out of her mouth or nose.
3. **nightmare :** (here) a very bad experience.

The text and **beyond**

KET ① **Comprehension check**

Choose the correct answer — A, B or C.

1 The two men who ask Shauna and Vanessa for directions
   A ☐ ask them to get into their car.
   B ☐ push them into their car.
   C ☐ get into Shauna and Vanessa's car.

2 The man with the sunglasses who crashed into the lorry in Chapter Four
   A ☐ was a friend of Steve.
   B ☐ was Steve's boss.
   C ☐ was a policeman.

3 Vanessa tries to send a text message to
   A ☐ Harminda.
   B ☐ the police.
   C ☐ a friend.

4 The car with Shauna, Vanessa and the criminals
   A ☐ stops close to the police car.
   B ☐ crashes into the police car.
   C ☐ passes the police car.

5 At the end of the chapter, Shauna feels that
   A ☐ they are still in danger.
   B ☐ she can't breathe easily.
   C ☐ they are out of danger.

② **Text messages**

This is the text message that Vanessa typed to Harminda. Write the full words of the abbreviated forms in the message below.

> U R IN DANGER. MEN TAKING US 2
> BUILDING IN EAST LONDON. B CAREFUL.
> MAN COMING 4 U. GO 2 POLICE. S&V

Text message abbreviation	Full word
U	1
R	2
2	3
B	4
4	5
S	6
V	7

In text messages, auxiliary verbs and articles are often omitted. Can you complete the following sentences from the text message?

A Some men .... taking us .... building in East London.

B .... man .... coming ....

C Go .... police.

3 Now match the following text messages to the correct full sentence

1 ☐ MEET U 2NITE AT 9.   4 ☐ R U FREE L8R AFTER CLASS?
2 ☐ R U OK?   5 ☐ C U ON FRI.
3 ☐ WANNA COME 2 MY   6 ☐ COFFEE B4 WORK?
        BDAY PARTY ON SAT?

A Are you free later after class?
B Are you OK?
C Do you want to come to my birthday party on Saturday?
D I'll see you on Friday.
E Let's meet tonight at 9 p.m..
F Shall we go for a coffee before work?

4 Rewrite the following text messages as full sentences.

1 JULIA COMING 4 DRINK 2NITE. WANNA COME 2?

....

2 WILL U B THERE B4 6?

....

3   C U L8R.

....

4   R U FREE 2 MEET 2NITE?

....

5 **Characters**

Match the sentences from Chapter Seven to the correct character below. There is one extra character who you don't need to use.

A Steve   **B** the driver   **C** Shauna   **D** Vanessa

1 ☐ 'What are you going to do with your ten per cent of the money?'
2 ☐ 'Did you see that crash between the lorry and the car with the plain-clothes police?'
3 ☐ 'They thought that was us in the accident!'
4 ☐ 'Of course we've got the money; we're not stupid!'
5 ☐ 'Hey! What are you doing! Give me that...!'
6 ☐ 'Leave her alone!'
7 ☐ 'You stupid woman!'

6 **Discussion**

Talk about these questions with a partner. Answer and ask these questions.

1   Do you think Shauna is a 'stupid woman' for pushing a man with a gun?
2   Who do you think the men work for? What's their job?
3   Harminda probably thinks that her friends have escaped with the money. How do you think she'll feel when she receives the message?

Before you read

1 **Prediction**

At the end of Chapter Seven, the nightmare is over for Vanessa and Shauna, but what about Harminda? Decide with a partner what you think happens to her in Chapter Eight.

Example: I think something's going to happen to Harminda - maybe Steve's boss will find her and hurt her. What do you think?

CHAPTER EIGHT Harminda Alone

'I'm sure they think I'm really stupid,' thought Harminda. 'And I am, because I believed them. "Spend time with your Dad before his operation," they said. They weren't worried about me spending time with Dad! The only thing they wanted was enough time to escape with the money!'

Vanessa didn't want to go to the police: she said that very clearly. But Shauna...

Shauna was different. At least, Harminda thought Shauna was different. She thought that after all this was over, they could be friends. But now she didn't know what to think any more.

'Maybe they've gone to get a drink or something to eat,' thought Harminda.

But she knew the truth.

Without Harminda there to stop her, Vanessa probably talked to Shauna about all the places Shauna could go on her honeymoon.

They could share the money. Half each. Fifty-fifty. That was

enough to go on honeymoon for over three months! Harminda could hear Vanessa. It was so easy to believe her. She was the perfect actress.

'Excuse me,' said a gentle voice, making Harminda jump. 'Sorry, I didn't want to frighten you.'

Harminda turned around and saw a young man. He was smiling kindly and when Harminda saw that his arm was in a plaster, [1] she started to relax.

'No, I'm sorry. How can I help?'

'Can you tell me the way to King's Cross station? I came here in an ambulance, but I don't know this part of London and I'm not sure how to get back home from here.'

'I don't know, but I've got a map in the car,' said Harminda.

She was about to put the key in the door when her mobile phone beeped. She had a new message. She took the phone out of her pocket and began to read: U R IN DANGER...

'No... this can't be happening... these things happen in films, not to people like me!' she thought, reading the message a second time.

She looked up slowly at the reflection of the man in the car window.

For a moment she couldn't believe what she saw. She was too frightened to breathe.

He was taking off the plaster! It was fake! [2] He didn't have a broken arm.

He was taking something out of his jacket...

Then Harminda realised what it was.

He was pulling out a gun.

1. **plaster :**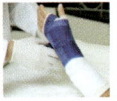

2. **fake :** not real.

The text and **beyond**

1 Comprehension check

Are these sentences true (T) or false (F)? Correct the false ones.

		T	F
1	Harminda believes that Vanessa and Shauna have taken the money for themselves.	☐	☐
2	Harminda thinks that Shauna persuaded Vanessa to take the money.	☐	☐
3	The young man who asks for directions doesn't really want to go to the station.	☐	☐
4	Harminda receives the text message that Vanessa sent in Chapter Seven.	☐	☐
5	The young man has a broken arm.	☐	☐
6	The young man has a knife in his jacket.	☐	☐

2 Vocabulary

Match the following expressions from Chapter Eight with their definitions below.

A ☐ Half each.   C ☐ This can't be happening...

B ☐ You made me jump.   D ☐ It was fake.

1 I wasn't expecting you and you surprised me.
2 It wasn't real.
3 It's impossible that this is happening.
4 50% for you, 50% for me.

3 Now decide which expression from the previous activity to use in the following situations.

1 ☐ The aeroplane you're on is going to crash.
2 ☐ You find out that the watch you paid a lot of money for is not a Rolex.
3 ☐ You want to share a pizza so that you and your friend have equal amounts.
4 ☐ You're reading a book and don't hear or see your friend come into the room until he speaks to you.

4 Characters

Match the two halves of the sentences from Chapter Eight.

1 ☐ 'Maybe they've gone   3 ☐ 'The only thing they wanted
2 ☐ 'I'm sure they think   4 ☐ 'These things happen in films,

A I'm really stupid.'
B not to people like me.'
C to get a drink or something to eat.'
D was enough time to escape with the money!'

Now discuss the following questions with a partner.

1 How do you think Harminda feels about Vanessa and Shauna at this point in the story?
2 Harminda believes that the young man needs directions to the station and tries to help him. Do you think that it is dangerous to help people in a situation like this?

Before you read

1 Prediction

Chapter Nine is the last chapter. Discuss the following predictions with a partner.

Harminda

1 She gets badly hurt.
2 She loses her baby.
3 She leaves Declan and stays in London with her family.

Vanessa

4 Her boyfriend comes back to her.
5 She is successful in her audition.

Shauna

6 She decides not to get married.

Harminda's father

7 He refuses to forgive her.
8 He dies during his operation.

CHAPTER **NINE** # Back Together

'Just a minute,' said Harminda. She looked around, careful not to alarm the gunman.

But the car park was dark and empty. There was nobody to ask for help.

In the glass of the car window she saw him raise the gun. Without thinking, she turned around and surprised him with a powerful kick. [1]

The man fell back, the gun dropped to the floor and went under the car. His head hit the side of the car and he fell to the ground.

Harminda didn't wait for him to wake up. She quickly dialled the number of the emergency services: 999.

Every second seemed like a year as she listened to the ringing, then a woman's voice answered, 'Emergency Services. Which

---

1. **kick** : if you kick someone or something, you hit them with your foot. Here *kick* is a noun.

service do you require: police, ambulance or fire?' and Harminda started to cry.

'Police please... hello? Police? There's a man with a gun. He wants to shoot me! I'm outside the Queen Elizabeth Hospital in London...'

But before she could finish telling the operator everything there was a loud bang... pain... and then, for Harminda, everything went black.

Harminda could see lights. Bright, white lights and her first thought was that she was dead. But then she felt someone touch her hand and her mother's sweet voice said her name.

Slowly, Harminda opened her eyes and her mother's face became clear.

'Mum?'

'It's alright, my darling...'

'What happened? Where am I?'

'You were shot, but you're going to be fine. You're in hospital.'

'What about my baby?' Harminda started to feel frightened.

'Your baby's fine,' Harminda saw that there were tears in her mother's eyes. But they were tears of happiness. 'I'm going to be a grandmother.'

Harminda looked around the room. Parindra was there. Even Shauna and Vanessa were there. Everyone except her Dad and Declan. Where were they?

'What day is it?' asked Harminda.

'It's Christmas Eve.'

'You're getting married! And what about your audition, Vanessa?'

'I got the part, of course! It's a thriller about some dangerous criminals. We're starting filming next week in France.'

Home for Christmas

'And I'm getting married in...' Shauna looked excitedly at the clock, 'about three hours from now... I really must go now — my mum is waiting for me with my dress — but I just wanted to see you before.'

'We wanted to know that you were OK,' smiled Vanessa.

There was only one more thing Harminda wanted to know, but she was also afraid of hearing the answer.

'Mum, how did Dad's operation go?' Harminda asked. But before Meena could answer, the door to Harminda's room opened.

'I hope this young man drives his car better than he does a wheelchair!' [1] said Harminda's father. Declan pushed him into the room and next to Harminda's bed.

'I love you,' Declan whispered [2] and kissed her gently on the lips.

Then Harminda's father took her hand, 'Harminda... I... when I heard you were shot, and in danger of dying, I thought about all those years. I realised that what is important is that you're happy. And if it is Declan,' he reached up for Declan's hand, 'that makes you happy, then I am happy.'

Seeing her tears, he looked suddenly worried. 'You are happy, aren't you?'

'Yes,' she said quietly. 'I am now... now that my family is back together.'

1. **wheelchair :**

2. **whispered :** said in a quiet voice.

The text and **beyond**

KET ① Comprehension check

Are these sentences 'Right' (A) or 'Wrong' (B)? If there is not enough information to answer 'Right' or 'Wrong' choose 'Doesn't say' (C). There is an example at the beginning (0).

0 Harminda finds someone in the car park to ask for help.
A Right   ⓑ Wrong   C Doesn't say

1 Harminda manages to phone for help.
A Right   B Wrong   C Doesn't say

2 The gunman shoots Harminda.
A Right   B Wrong   C Doesn't say

3 Harminda knows that her baby is a boy.
A Right   B Wrong   C Doesn't say

4 Vanessa's audition didn't go well for her.
A Right   B Wrong   C Doesn't say

5 Harminda's boyfriend arrived in London the previous day.
A Right   B Wrong   C Doesn't say

6 Harminda's father changes his opinion about his daughter's situation.
A Right   B Wrong   C Doesn't say

② Characters

Put the words in each of the following sentences from Chapter Nine in the right order.

1 about/baby/my/What

.... ?

2 a/be/going/grandmother/I'm/to

....

3 course/got/I/of/part/the

......................................, ... !

4 about/And/getting/now/I'm/married/three/in/hours/from

....

5 Dad's/did/go/how/Mum/operation

........................., ... ?

6 a/better/car/does/drives/he/his/hope/I/man/than/this/
wheelchair/young

.... !

7 am/And/Declan/happy/happy/I/if/is/it/makes/that/then/you

...., ...

Now match each of the sentences with one of the characters below.
Some characters say more than one sentence. There is one extra
character who you don't need to use.

A ☐☐ Declan   **D** ☐☐ Harminda

B ☐☐ Harminda's father   **E** ☐☐ Harminda's mother

C ☐☐ Shauna   **F** ☐☐ Vanessa

3 Discussion

Decide with a partner how each of the above characters feels at the
end of the story.

Example: **Student A:** I think Harminda feels worried about her
baby and her father. What do you think?

Student B: Yes, I agree, but then she feels happy when
she knows that her father accepts Declan.

4 Listening

999 – the emergency services

track 15

Listen to the following calls to the emergency services and decide
which service(s) the caller needs — police, ambulance or fire.

Caller	Service/s needed
1	
2	
3	
4	
5	

5 **British Christmas traditions**

The protagonists finally get home for Christmas! Here are seven very typical elements of a British Christmas. On your own, number them in the boxes from 1 (what you think is the oldest) to 7 (what you think is the most recent). Compare your ideas, and only then read the paragraphs that come after them to find out the answers!

☐ Santa Claus   ☐ Roast turkey   ☐ Christmas presents

☐ his red and white costume   ☐ Roast potatoes   ☐ the Christmas tree

☐ Christmas cards

The Christmas tree, which has origins in pre-Christian times, was used in Northern Europe to celebrate Christmas before it came to Britain. Some rich British families used a Christmas tree at the beginning of the eighteenth century but Prince Albert, the German husband of Queen Victoria, brought a Christmas tree to Windsor Castle in 1841, a year after he married Victoria. After that it became very popular.

The Spanish found turkeys in Mexico in 1518, and by 1530 these birds were common in Europe. The word 'turkey' was first used for them in 1541. These big birds are not connected to Turkey, but there was another, smaller bird called a 'guinea fowl' which was imported into Europe through Turkey, and people at first confused the two birds, which were both new to Europe. A document mentions turkey as a Christmas food for the first time in 1575.

Santa Claus comes from Saint Nicholas, a fourth-century Christian bishop from Myra in southern Turkey, famous for his miracles and generosity. In northern Europe people started to give each other presents on his feast day, 6 January. In Holland they abbreviated his name to Sinterklaas (Saint Nicholas), and Dutch emigrants took this name to the USA, where it gradually changed to Santa Claus. Nowadays Santa Claus and Father Christmas are the same thing, although they come from different traditions – the south of Europe and the north of Europe.

Some kinds of cards existed before Christmas cards; for example, cards for Saint Valentine's Day. But an Englishman, Henry Cole, produced the first commercial Christmas cards in 1843.

At the Roman feast of the Saturnalia (17-24 December) the Romans gave each other small gifts, called 'strenae'. But it only became common for people to give presents in the 1870s and 1880s in the commercial boom in the USA. Before this, if people gave small presents, they didn't wrap them in paper. But at this time shops wrapped the presents that people bought in paper that advertised their shops. This was the beginning of the custom of wrapping presents in special paper.

Before the 1850s, Santa Claus/Father Christmas usually wore furs or green-coloured winter clothes. But in 1885 he wore red and white in a 1885 Christmas card; this became popular, and it became the usual costume for Santa Claus when a series of adverts for Coca-Cola in the 1930s showed him in the red and white colours of Coca-Cola.

The English explorer Sir Walter Raleigh brought white potatoes back to England from the New World in 1586 and planted them on his farms in Ireland. Another kind of potato from the New World is the sweet potato, but the English did not import them.

6 **Speaking: festivals**

Describe an important festival to a visitor to your country or region. It could be Christmas, or another festival.

Mention the origins, and what people do and eat.

Tell him/her where some of the typical elements come from.

1 Picture summary

Look at the pictures, put them in order and say what is happening in each one.

2 Characters

Who said or thought what? Match the correct phrase with the characters. You can use some names more than once.

Harminda (H)
Vanessa (V)
Harminda's father (F)
Mr O'Flaherty (O)

Shauna (S)
Chrissie (C)
Harminda's mother (M)
One of the criminals (CR)

1. ☐ 'I have to get to London as soon as possible. My Dad's ill.'
2. ☐ 'I'm getting married in three days.'
3. ☐ 'And I've got a very important audition!'
4. ☐ 'Mr O'Flaherty will be pleased.'
5. ☐ 'That car was reserved, you stupid girl!'
6. ☐ 'Love is for idiots.'
7. ☐ 'Don't forget your briefcase.'
8. ☐ 'That'll never work.'
9. ☐ 'There are hundreds of thousands of euros here!'
10. ☐ 'Do you realise what a difference this money could make to my ... to our lives?'
11. ☐ 'I don't know ... my fiancé and I really want a honeymoon.'
12. ☐ 'They wanted me to marry someone else ... somebody they chose.'
13. ☐ 'I don't want you here. You made your decision. Please leave!'
14. ☐ 'I'm sure they think I'm really stupid.'
15. ☐ 'Can you tell me the way to King's Cross station?'
16. ☐ 'I'm going to be a grandmother.'
17. ☐ I got the part, of course!'
18. ☐ 'I hope this young man drives his car better than he does a wheelchair!'

Key to Exit Test

1 **H** 1; **G** 3; **F** 4; **B** 5; **A** 6; **C** 7; **D** 8; **E** 9.

2 1 H; 2 S; 3 V; 4 C; 5 O; 6 V; 7 H; 8 S; 9 H; 10 V; 11 S; 12 H; 13 F; 14 H; 15 CR; 16 M; 17 V; 18 F.

This reader uses the **EXPANSIVE READING** approach, where the text becomes a springboard to improve language skills and to explore historical background, cultural connections and other topics suggested by the text.

The new structures introduced in this step of our **READING & TRAINING** series are listed below. Naturally, structures from lower steps are included too. For a complete list of structures used over all the six steps, see *The Black Cat Guide to Graded Readers*, which is also downloadable at no cost from our website, blackcat-cideb.com.

The vocabulary used at each step is carefully checked against vocabulary lists used for internationally recognised examinations.

Step **One A2**

All the structures used in the previous levels, plus the following:

Verb tenses
Present Simple
Present Continuous
Past Simple
Past Continuous
Future reference: Present Continuous; *going to*; *will*; Present Simple
Present Perfect Simple: indefinite past with *ever, never* (for experience)

Verb forms and patterns
Regular and common irregular verbs
Affirmative, negative, interrogative
Imperative: 2nd person; *let's*
Passive forms: Present Simple; Past Simple
Short answers
Infinitives after verbs and adjectives
Gerunds (verb + *-ing*) after prepositions and common verbs

Gerunds (verb + *-ing*) as subjects and objects

Modal verbs
Can: ability; requests; permission
Could: ability; requests
Will: future reference; offers; promises; predictions
Would … like: offers, requests
Shall: suggestions; offers
Should (present and future reference): advice
May (present and future reference): possibility
Must: personal obligation
Mustn't: prohibition
Have (got) to: external obligation
Need: necessity

Types of clause
Co-ordination: *but; and; or; and then*
Subordination (in the Present Simple or Present Continuous) after verbs such as: *to be sure; to know; to think; to believe; to hope; to say; to tell*
Subordination after: *because, when, if* (zero and 1st conditionals)
Defining relative clauses with: *who, which, that*, zero pronoun, *where*

Other
Zero, definite and indefinite articles
Possessive *'s* and *s'*
Countable and uncountable nouns
Some, any; much, many, a lot; (a) little, (a) few; all, every; etc.
Order of adjectives
Comparative and superlative of adjectives (regular and irregular)
Formation and comparative/superlative of adverbs (regular and irregular)

Available at Step **One**: